Through My Eyes

Lisa Newton

Presentation by *BookLeaf Publishing*

Web: www.bookleafpub.com

E-mail: info@bookleafpub.com

ISBN: 9789357615716

First edition 2022

To my children.

PREFACE

I fell in love with poetry as a child and have written it for as long as I can remember. I believe that poetry comes from the soul. When I write, it is like therapy for me. My writing takes on many forms and is very free flowing, I don't follow any guidelines or have any set limitations for myself before I begin. I get inspired by the people and experiences in my life.

Acceptance

When you don't fit the image that society deems
appealing,
You often want to hide yourself from others.
This causes you to have a very empty feeling,
And make you want to run and hide beneath the
covers.
When people hand out judgments and give
people labels,
It puts them in a place of hurt and shame.
Be careful what you say for life often turns the
tables,
You may find yourself at the losing end of the
game.

Addiction

Addiction isn't something that you choose to suffer from,
It doesn't matter who or where you are it can effect anyone.
It's a never ending illness that you have to fight with everyday.
It slowly creeps up on you and then never goes away.
It seeps into your daily life and changes what you do.
Soon you start to forget yourself and other people too.
You'll do things that you never thought you were capable of,
You will hurt the ones around you, especially the ones you love.
You loose control of what you think, what you feel and what you know,
You don't care what you need to do or say or how low you need to go.
All you ever think about is how to get to that next high,
You will do anything you can think of, you will beg and steal and lie.

Your body starts to need it just to function
through the day,
Just a little bit you'll tell yourself to chase the
pain away.
You try to stop again and again but it creeps
back in your life,
It's like a never ending cycle of pain and shame
and strife.
It's sad to think that some believe some choose
this way to live,
To spend one day without the pain there isn't
anything I wouldn't give.

Anything Anytime, Anywhere

If you ever need to talk, know I'm here just for
you.
If you need a shoulder to cry on know I've got
that too.
When the front porch seems lonely and there's
an empty chair,
Know that I am here for you, Anything,
Anytime, Anywhere.
When the work is hard and the kids are loud,
And you need a hand, but you feel too proud
Please don't hesitate to share,
Know that I am here for you, Anything,
Anytime, Anywhere.
When the days are short and the nights are long
When our hair is grey and our youth is gone,
There will never be a time when I don't care
Know that I am here for you, Anything,
Anytime, Anywhere.

Blanket of Blue

Somebody's child whose could it be?
I looked into your eyes and I knew it was me.
All of the pain and all of the tears,
Were replaced with the thought of the next fifty
years.
Somebody's mother? Responsible? Strong?
Was it possible that once, God could be wrong?
How could I give you all that you need?
Could I teach you to walk, talk and read?
Make sure you're happy, healthy and care for?
Give you every opportunity and open all doors?
Could I give you the knowledge to know right
from wrong?
So you could grow up secure, kind and strong?
Instantly, it was as clear as a bell!
Things would be fine, it would all work out well.
I looked down at you with a tearful eye,
it was my duty, my purpose in life.
There was no mistake, God gave you to me.
A gift so precious it was meant to be.
You are my pride, my joy my SON!
The best years of my life had finally begun.
I wanted to sing, I felt I could fly,
But all I could do was just sit there and cry.

So much emotion, so much Love, so much to
do!
Who knew that So much could be wrapped up in
a blanket of blue?

Broken Promises

Why does it have to hurt so bad?
Why does it have to be this hard?
Why cant I stop my heart from hurting and
theses tears from burning and leave this dark?

You didn't have to lie to me.
You didn't have to walk away.
You didn't have to break my heart over and over
again, each and every single day.

I thought we were meant to be together.
I thought we would stand the test of time.
I thought it would be you and me forever and
ever our souls eternally intertwined.

You're never going to be able to fix this.
You're never going to make this right.
You're never going to be able to take it all back,
put us back together and hold me tight.

I just can't accept that it's over.
It hurts to much to say goodbye.
I just don't know how to move on without you
I will love you until the day that I die.

Christmas Hope

It's hard to believe that it's that time of year,
The decorations are up and the snows almost here.
People are shopping, there are crowds everywhere,
But under our small Christmas tree it's just bare.
It's hard to remember all the excitement you feel,
When you believe in something so strong it seems
real.
Where there are men made of snow and reindeer that
fly,
And you had no idea one day that magic would die.
It's hard to imagine a sleigh without bells,
Or a toy, or a present not wrapped up by elves.
It's hard to hang stockings without any cheer,
Or make resolutions for the upcoming year.
It's hard to forget that the bills are not paid,
But the children's wish lists are already made.
They've written to Santa and mailed off their letter,
And all I can do is just pray it gets better.
This year Dear Santa, I have a wish of my own.
Please keep my kids fed, and keep us in our home.
I don't need new slippers, a new robe or soap,
This year my Christmas wish is for hope.

Despair

Sometimes it's a struggle just to get out of my bed.
It's so very hard to fight what's inside my own head.
When words just can't describe the pain,
And tears are falling just like the rain.
There's just a great big hole inside,
And nowhere left for me to hide.
It's such a hopeless feeling, when you know you're all alone.
When you search your entire life but nothing feels like home.
Some days you think it's pointless just to carry on
And other days you just sit and wait until the feelings gone.
Someday I hope they'll find a cure for the illness in my head.
Until that day, I just stay safe inside my cozy bed.

Forgiveness

We always hurt the ones we love, it happens to us all.
We don't always intend to do so, but sometimes we take a fall.
Sometimes we just need a break, or have run out of things to do.
Sometimes it's just a case of hurt them before they can hurt you!
It's hard to take a look inside and see where your heart is at.
We all play a part in our own lives and sometimes we forget that.
Forgiveness isn't easy, is so very hard to do.
It is less about the other person and more to do with you.
Relationships aren't simple they take a lot of care
However if you nurture them, it's worth it if you dare.

Hole in My Heart

There's a hole in my heart and it's tearing me apart.
I can't remember when I felt so blue.
There's a dream in my soul and it doesn't feel whole,
And it's not sure what it's supposed to do.
Where it's gone, I don't know
How to save it, I'm not sure
Will it ever return?
How much more I can endure?
It's an old dream damaged and broken,
Like unanswered prayers; wishes unspoken.
Still I long to make it come true,
Cause it reminds me of the girl I once knew.
Where she's gone, I don't know,
How to save her I'm not sure,
Will she ever return?
How much more I can endure?
She's a good girl, lost and alone
And she's so scared can't find her way back home.
She doesn't know if she can hold on,
She feels like all hope is gone.
Where it's gone, I don't know,
How to save it, I'm not sure,
Will it ever return?
How much more I can endure?

Letting Go

I used to be the type of person who held on to things too tight,
Afraid that if I let them go, I'd lose a piece of myself too.
I would try so hard just to make sure that everything was right,
That I became someone that I no longer knew.
You can't force people to want to stay in your life,
Or make an effort to show how much they care for you.
Sometimes you have to let go of the things that cause you strife,
And you may find that you find yourself again when you do.

Life

As life goes on so many things change,
And they may not turn out how we thought they
would.
Sometimes people and places become strange,
But we wouldn't change them if we could.
Our journey will have many paths for us to
choose,
On which we will have many decisions to make.
Sometimes we will win and sometimes we will
lose,
But there will be lessons from each we will take.
There will be times that we struggle and times
that we thrive,
And times when we don't know our way.
There may even be days it hurts to be alive,
But hopefully those days don't stay.
Our bodies will age and our minds will get slow,
And our memories will become hard to recall.
We still might have questions but we will know,
That in the end it was worth it all.

Lost and Alone

When all I feel is emptiness it's hard to carry on,
With every breath, unsteadiness all my hope is
gone.
Dark shadows suffocate me, there is agony in
every breath.
A wave of uncertainty looms like impending
death.
I'm drowning in sorrow, there is nothing but
despair,
I can't even remember what it feels like to care.
I no longer have ambition or the willingness to
strive,
I long to remember what it means to feel alive.
I'm lost and alone in a world of my own,
I can't seem to find a light or a way to come
back home.
I see a life in front of me waiting to be endured
I'm paralyzed with the thought that I can never
be cured.

Mental Illness

When you suffer from an illness that nobody can
see,
It often feels like you need to prove your pain.
Constantly being judged is a lonely place to be,
With so much to lose and very little to gain.
Family and friends think they know what is best,
They give advice and opinions and what for.
When most days you are too tired to even rest,
You feel guilty for not doing a little more.
Years of trying new drugs and therapy hinder
hope,
That you will find a life free of doubt and
sorrow.
So you learn to modify and do your best just to
cope,
So that you may live with the promise of
tomorrow.

Mom

There will never be enough words to tell you what
you mean to me.
There will never be enough time to spend with you.
There will never be enough days to say you love me.
There will never be enough ways to thank you for all
you do.
I will never be ready to live one day without you.
I will never be prepared to accept when your gone.
I will never forget all the little things that you do.
I will never believe we'll be apart long.
There will always be love in my life because of you.
There will always be joy in my heart.
There will always be memories old and new.
There will always be laughter even when we're apart.
I will always be thankful for all that you've given me.
I will Always be grateful for the time that we shared.
I will always know how precious life can be.
I will always remember how much you cared.

Music

Music is the medicine that my soul deeply longs for,
It makes me feel things that I've never felt before.
I can hear a song and be taken to a place of my own.
When I hear a song I love it's like I feel at home.
Nothing else speaks to me like the way that music will,
It can bring up emotions that I haven't thought of still.
Music can make memories or bring up ones you've shelved,
It can bring us close to others and help us express ourselves.
A melody can soothe my soul and bring me peace of mind,
And take me to a place where I can leave my worries behind.
A song can open up your heart and set your soul on fire,
It can bring out your darkest fear or deepest desire.
Music can transform your pain your joy your deepest sadness,
It is my favourite way to navigate through the madness.

Never Give Up

I have never seen anyone with so much heart
and drive,
So young and determined and so much alive.
From the time that you were born, you have
always been that way.
When you want something there is nothing that
will lead you astray.
I have no doubt in my mind that you will go
very far.
You are my pride and joy, my little shooting star.
I know you will do great things know matter
what you do.
Remember to take time to enjoy the little things
life offers too.
Sometimes you'll need to look inside to find
your own visions.
You have all the strength you need to make the
right decisions.
I will always be here to guide you, no matter
what you do.
Just know how proud and grateful I am and how
much I love you.

October

Pumpkins on porches and leaves on the ground
Autumn colours beginning to appear all around
Apple picking and hay rides and the smell of
sweet corn
Waking up to the very first frost in the morn
Warm cozy blankets and hot apple cider
Camp songs become ghost stories by fire
Corn mazes and costumes and candy galore
Ghosts and goblins and lots of folklore
Whether you love it or it causes you fear
For me it is the very best time of year!

Somebody That I Used To Know

When I was young I was foolish, I didn't know
how life could be.
Now when I look in the mirror there's a stranger
starring back at me.
There is an emptiness inside of her and I know
she longs to be free.
So full of pain and loneliness and it hurts her
just to breathe.
She doesn't feel whole any longer,
And all she prays for is to be stronger,
And remember who is she?

Sugar and Spice

Sugar and spice and everything nice is not what
I am made of.
Hopes and fears, laughter and tears that's what I
am made of.
Thoughts and prayers, doubt and cares that's
what I am made of.
Anger and sadness, chaos and madness that's
what I am made of.
Sarcasm and attitude, peace and gratitude that's
what I am made of.
Hugs and kisses, dreams and wishes, that's what
I am made of.
Aches and pains, loses and gains that's what I
am made of.
Love and sorrow and the chance of tomorrow
that's what I am made of.

'Tis the Season

Snows falling, carollers calling,
Decorations on the streets.
Bells ringing, children singing,
Lights twinkling on the trees.
Stockings hanging, drums are banging,
Presents wrapped with pretty bows.
Fire roasting, chestnuts toasting,
Jack Frost's nipping at your nose.
Couples dancing, reindeer's prancing,
Mistletoe hung from up above.
Santa's jolly, boughs of holly,
'Tis the season of love.

Where My Demons Hide

Inside every one of us a little demon hides,
And sometimes we just need to let it out.
It could be on the surface or buried deep inside,
But eventually it will start to scream and shout.
It may slowly creep up on you, or may come out
in a blast,
Or it may linger and control what you will do.
It could disappear and leave you just as fast,
And you might never know what you thought
you knew.
Our demons are there to remind us of the things
that make us real,
They come from things that happen as we learn.
Everything we go through our soul will surely
feel,
And sometimes it leaves a scar so deep you'll
feel a burn.
This burn will start a fire where the demon starts
to grow,
How big it grows depends on how much pain we
feed it.
How to destroy the demon you may never really
know,
But the more you let it out to play the less you
feel defeated.

Printed in the USA
CPSIA information can be obtained
at www.ICGtesting.com
LVHW010928101123
763485LV00091B/3928